My Photo Album

poems by

Rubeena Anjum

Finishing Line Press
Georgetown, Kentucky

My Photo Album

Copyright © 2023 by Rubeena Anjum
ISBN 979-8-88838-285-1 First Edition
All rights reserved under International and Pan-American Copyright Conventions. No part of this book may be reproduced in any manner whatsoever without written permission from the publisher, except in the case of brief quotations embodied in critical articles and reviews.

ACKNOWLEDGMENTS

The Ekphrastic Review: "She wears a Pearl Earring"
The Ekphrastic Review: "Masks Hide Even More"
Word City Literary Journal: "Histograms"
Word City Literary Journal: "Climate Change"

Publisher: Leah Huete de Maines
Editor: Christen Kincaid
Cover Art: Rubeena Anjum
Author Photo: Rubeena Anjum
Cover Design: Elizabeth Maines McCleavy

Order online: www.finishinglinepress.com
               also available on amazon.com

Author inquiries and mail orders:
Finishing Line Press
P. O. Box 1626
Georgetown, Kentucky 40324
U. S. A.

Table of Contents

1. Photo Album
2. Ishmael
3. Maryam
4. Adam
5. Gardens
6. Savants and Savages
7. Silence 9/11
8. Marylin Monroe
9. Monet's Water Lilies
10. Humphrey Fellows
11. Preacher
12. Sufi
13. Beggar's Lamp
14. Begging Bowl
15. Xenophobes
16. Witnesses
17. Immigrant
18. No Knock Warrant
19. Chainsaw
20. Messengers
21. Pizza people
22. Okra
23. Norma
24. Cart Pusher
25. Daily Wagers
26. Grackles
27. Beetle
28. Uncle Darrin
29. Mocking Bird
30. Jillana
31. Blue Whale
32. Sepphora, Quite Contrary
33. Uncle Ben
34. Emma
35. Phantom and Opera
36. Albert
37. Gold
38. Ali Sadpara

39. Janice
40. Twins
41. Grandparents
42. Crowd
43. Sattar Edhi Baba
44. Michael
45. Sunflowers
46. Card Players
47. Molly
48. Forbes List
49. Histograms
50. Chocolates
51. Alijah
52. Alijah and Amy
53. Anne
54. Picasso Paints Pandemic
55. So Many Names
56. Myra
57. Earthquake 2/6/2023
58. Sci-fi Film
59. Pearls
60. Miracle
61. Hakan
62. Dad
63. Mom
64. Mama's Shirt
65. Odd Couple
66. Crescent Eyes
67. Downside
68. Rex and Ruth
69. Silverware
70. Guru Says
71. First Love
72 .Pearl Earring
73. Doorway
74. Journey by Jeep
75. Isabelle
76. Sushi Lover
77. Masks and Me
78. Sheba, Sybil and Sappho
79. Last Photo

dedicated to my daughter, Dr. Aaisha Khan

1. Photo Album

logged in each frame—a story
as life cartwheels calm and chaos
losses weighing heavy; gains adding up
memories choreograph sequences:

those loved and gone, those still here
those just met, faces shaped as promises
those not seen nor heard, those kept
as scars healed, as wishes tied as buds

in sepals; in arranging flowers
the pain of being plucked saved
in shifting visions, as years move
suppose—if stars rebel, refuse to shine

and the darkening night seeks help
how hopes resize to fit the sky
photos in my album reflect much more
even more, I don't mean to tell

2.   Ishmael

bullets wheeling blind
charcoal-colored crags spurt blood
                azure tones red
alone he sleeps, helmet masking face
he is my brother, named after Ishmael
son of Abraham, the one born for sacrifice

putting on a saddlebag, he promised pa
he will tend the ranch, tame horses
be home before the spring festival
how can the heart answer duty calls
        as he fell
hours died on his wristwatch

without a casket
in alien soil, chest wound-crested
for wars unknown, for reasons not known
unknown soldier breathes his last
harvest moon knows how
            much life loved him

3.　　Maryam

fighting continued for days
leaving himself at the line of control
the martyr came home as a news
　　　　heartbroken mother said
those who die fighting for a cause
　　　　　　live forever

my father, a compulsive patriot
for his country's defense, he had three sons
lucky was one, saluted with guns
　　now gone, gone forever
Maryam, wearing a crown of thorns
tears rolling lifelong

　　　　　　lover, husband, a friend
now gone, gone forever
hands down her heart, she hugged
their unborn child　　　sobs echoing
wedding vows till death do us part
death came　　disguised as a war

4. Adam

inhaling phosphorous,
fog silhouettes maneuvers
mouthing litanies; the buttons pushed
        missiles explode

he followed orders
Adam loved his flag and held it high
for the flag, he fought, he died
in a flag wrapped—boxes lined up

and those downed, those remembered
because they loved—they loved
their flags and saving flags
      they disappeared

buddies who shared fags at school
      because smokes are thrills, they
        never read omens printed on packs
          smoking kills

5.   Gardens

those fighting here; those there
on each loss, a wreath laid
flowers know how soldiers die

in orange-blue sunsets of peace
dealers plan weaponry sales, and
warlords merging corporate chains

in plants, where ammunition made
to cap each bullet with a rose
everywhere gardens grow

6.   Savants and Savages

under the aging sky, wolves lick moist wounds
as firing starts anew, wild and intense
tracks littered with death, without recompense
air spitting blood—the same old bell resounds

busts breaking down, brass bullets spinning rounds
slogans scull spoils and freedom mere pretense
those set free choosing more arms for defense
yet again, rebel lords walk the prized grounds

as flags fly, wheels run, cogs roll fast, exchange
of rags to robes and wealth robbed thru ravages
those weak, down on knees and power, so strange
it converts savants into savages

Does revolution bring a striking change?
Yes, rage makes people suffer for ages.

7.   Silence 9/11

back then, misty morn—signals blinked, street bull
yawned, leaves caught in sunny wafts reeled fine
no showers predicted, clear blue sky
wrapped in slightly nippy late-summer swirls

as usual, overseeing flights of migrant birds
gently, both ways, crisscross, the Hudson flowed
—the hour struck zilch, bellowing clouds puffed fires
screams dialing 911 swarmed on audiovisuals 9/11

stately towers smashed spines—tongues
spitted red, each bud tasted vintage venom(s)
the sun-coiled rattlesnake rolled raw
in mushroom smokes of dark convictions

feathered petals rained on quivering grey ashes
in chemo-therapies, hearts reincarnated souls
—silence after a thunderstorm is not sleep
charred steel relics gracing parks assure

trials are tides, be brave, Manhattan bells ring loud
in remembrance, never—underestimate hope
gently, the river flows, bald eagles gain heights, ones
who rescued lives; in ebbing waters, their names glow

8.   Marylin Monroe

grief-stricken sky
pain and hurt written in bold
swallows flog themselves
weep, wail, vanish in throngs
wound-red crimson slits
wrists wreathed in dripping blood
light fading from inside
sinking sun commits suicide

half traversed, half ahead
tinnitus spreads waves around
weary boats shredding waters
her thoughts snitched by sounds
yellow snakes bending blue
struck with bouts of jilted love
self-eclipsed in flashlights
Marylin Monroe stands alone

night means nightmares
muffled shrieks have regrets trailed
a morphed moon whisking qualms
stars willingly wear black
rusty bridge catching fire, smoke
weaving tomorrow's headlines
paparazzi scavenging screams
out there, she needs help

9. Monet's Water Lilies

shining stars fell, landed in a pool
dived down, rolled in mud and sand
felt the warmth beneath the bosoms
played with mermaids, changed forms
swam up as whiffs of colors whipped
on a wooden palette by some wizard
blossoms woke up with a magic wand

reflecting light with enticing grace
foggy clouds conjure familiar images
serene surface replicating azure skies
tawny shores seized in mirrors of sand
ash gray rubble at the bottom hides
wishes lost with coins in latent ponds
anchored in stems promises survive

dipped in yellow gold, muted silver
conceal the fate of unfinished dreams
buds in a peachy pink and hazy white
purple eyes cast shades of disbelief
fables live in specks of viridian green
subtle cerise islands of passion drift
water lilies are poems in the making

10. Humphrey Fellows

friends from the world over
198 of them gathered at Capitol Hill
in a feast of colors, the kind I fit in
and they with me, when pelts pulled
neath layers of lard are veins
ichor filled but in dins of dissonance
biases pushed in lungs and livers—

manifestoes, loyalties, recognitions
resound, resonate taglines
not one of us, not one of us
mantras reset boundary lines—
bile cast in bricks and bricks arched
in holy places: beliefs strung in rhymes
and for those who differ, rosaries count

not one of us, not one of us—
souls dowsed in rituals; they char
on skewers of devotion {they who say, No}
Humphrey fellows! Echo tremors till
springs flow from fissures—waters cure
sore, sour, swollen tongues—listen how
voices blend air into mantras of empathy

11. Preacher

pressing prayers in plastic beads
a preacher—the most respected
Pandit, Priest, Cohen, Imam, Guru
narratives enveloped in virtues

he nailed my soul with insularity
as he said, I did, and in pleasing him
in tallying faults, others may have
what little faith I had, *I lost*

knowing there are fights, I'll never win
because thinking is a sin, I have swirled
in hula-hoops of faith: where mediators go
I take U-turns to   seek God solo

12. Sufi

I have to think again
is my fascination with me
a new kind of invocation?

putting myself in the center
circumambulating a figure, Me
have I become a solipsistic Sufi?

lover, beloved, and rival
three divided selves within
all conspire, make sure I love me

in relationships, I want more
therefore, I propose litmus tests
of doubt, debate, and disbelief

13. Beggar's Lamp

bent old toothless woman wrapped
in rags, her crooked cane dragging
swollen feet for years in callous streets
often without meals, the homeless slept

dusk blanketing dark the sky, devoutly
she watched townsfolk carrying costly lamps
for light offerings to Buddha on Mount Sumeru
how she wished to be there—she begged

the vendor to cut off her greyish-white braid
less than an ounce, the dusty hair weighed
in exchange, he spilled a few kerosene drops
in her little clay lamp, wick moist enough

to spark a tiny flame that drowned
in rivers of light flowing back and forth
on terraces where disciples sat in awe
of Gautama's words impacting hearts—

suddenly, a contemptuous wind blew
leaping lamps lost light to smoke and soot
in darkness then, what illumed the long night
was a sun shining inside the beggar's lamp

14. Begging Bowl

my hand, a begging bowl, throw
a kind word of mercy, pity for my soul

what I said and did to gain in ledgers
is loss inked in guilt and pain and shame

now, I know why so famed and rich
my cards can't buy—a strand of light

to walk me thru the valley of the shadow
because I played to win no matter what

because if others failed, I thrived, this choice
my flaw, I beg forgiveness before it's late

15. Xenophobes

bullets shredding willows
shots straddle in silencers
<u>this place belongs to us,</u> the slogans
are scripts controlling decisions—
from baby cots, the toys fall
floors absorb screams

    xenophobes wearing masks
triggering Führer hate
replay scenes of a holocaust
pyres lit, houses grounding zero
these are photos from Daily Times
       of rituals staged at night

patrol cars rushing, flashing blue
they see nothing; hear nothing
roofs no more and proofs burnt
reporters stream live, as usual
race—color—religion—origin
in postmortems—cure—not found

16. Witnesses

afraid
of what might happen to them

        as doors locked for safety
        mouths latched securely
        keys hidden in closed eyes

witnesses have pushed their tongues
in pits as deep as caves

17. Immigrant

a drop of olive oil spilled
in water never blends or bonds
unsteadily it seeks space

when the   glow of dawn
treks thru it   in light and colors
a spectrum   settling in a sphere

it never sinks but stays
it sails, it swims, it prevails
and not denying what it is

it brings shine to Mississippi waves
a rainbow pearl in the river, Rukhsana
now Rosanne dives with minnows n whales

18. No Knock Warrant

each day, trigger-trained hands
load the same savage games
shoot and shout, calling names

no-knock warrant bang doors
pulls, pushes, applies force
law flaws without remorse

targets ticked, dot on clock
they enter, raid, invade
looking glass absorbs shock:

pressed against the hard wall
black, brown, and white bodies fall
Amir Locke, count him too

19. Chainsaw

how the chainsaw works
dying till death is daring
fallen trees can tell

20. Messengers

as old texts record, as savants infer
Buddha had darker skin than Abraham
Zoroaster and Jesus were olive-colored
Confucius, a lighter shade of brown or beige
and Guru Nanak mud toned as Hindu deities

waiting for Moses to ascend as if—
he'll lift his staff, and much like his hand
all bodies bleached white; creeds dyed one
such fallacies no more, look around—See
how nature celebrates miscellany

the black and white in each chi
as in night and day mint hues and dyes
to shape the cyclic wheel of life
as the zodiac determines soul and body
skins, mere wrappers: inside is love—love

21. Pizza People

iris eyes absorb assorted colors
infused herbs, oregano, basil, and thyme
spinach, black olives, brown mushrooms

red, green, and orange bell peppers
pearly garlic, Himalayan salt sprinkled evenly
on Roma tomatoes and onions sauteed fair to tan

Okeechobee sugar added to Montana wheat
leavening yeast in hierarchies, Mozzarella
and Parmesan drip-paint diced veggies

dough baked in 500C of a wood-fired oven
the odds inside and tugs tied to fiery waves
bond and blend; create a Pollock painting

in a pageant of hues, ranch dressings
squirting streaks on creamy sauces packed
in lavish zesty bites—wahoo tastes divine

since ages golden gateway docks
immigrant aromas—IDs rinsed in virgin oils
visions swirled in a bowl: dreams pot melted

spread on a rounded stone—that delight
inviting all to cherish life is American Pizza
toppings autograph: we, the people

22. Okra

in oil-heated pan
okra loses slime and stirred

with ingredients

blend makes this veg dish divine
life's recipe is the same

23.   Norma

she works in Uncle Darrin's diner
with shiny eyes, her life, she shares:

I have tweezed my fears, tweaked
unwanted hair on my upper lip
trimmed me for a job, edited full
my CV—qualified GMAT
(*Gorgeously Mad as Tested*)

a smiling look, a new hairdo
glossy lips eager to oblige
waiting tables, opening bottles
counting tips, not so many
mopping fairy tales from floors
hoping I kiss one hell of a toad

regulars making tidal waves
music drowning routine worries
serving dishes, high-heeled pumps
pack more hurts in narrowed toes
dabbing powder on my face, I start
serving tables over again

setting aside slumbering chairs
dumping garbage, emptying bins
drawing shades, putting off lights,
I walk on the high-end NYC street
like coal in a diamond mine
I know someday, I will shine

24.   Cart Pusher

a cart pusher pulls his day, unaware
of how workers raised slabs for Pharaohs' tombs
how the slackened lashed and chained—hours
clocked in, soul-locked

in carts zigzagging plans of keeping up
with college, learning what's right; blurring
it with wrongs and whatever—head down, hands
busy, feet hurrying: carts dragging on tracks

of appetite till harbors reached where ships
sail smooth, rain n thunder claps symphonies, stars
steer fire streets: it happens in dreams—head
down, hands busy, feet hurrying,

swallow cycle continues—customers come
and go; he gathers loose litter—bins cleared
bags replaced and doing so, no one notices
how hard the lad works. Tom Thumb

lifted by a raven, gulped by a cow, a giant, a fish—
he played with mice and cats and flew on the wings
of butterflies; he died bitten by a high-tech bug
the fairy tale has no sequel—soon, the bi-pedal

Humanoids will stream carts; the wheels
setting straight a geometric world: race, origin, kind
spun in evolution, those who correspond—will live
head held high, Rambo clocks out of a spider's web

25. Daily Wagers

working in marts as big as ships, they
stand and sell, lift loads, walk trollies in—
circuit cameras watch buyers come and go
lunch break over, back to aching backs
happiness means

                paychecks after 15 days

fragile hearts on a needle ticking clockwise
shearing needs to make the most of less
buying monthly payment plans, putting
necks in leashes, free markets whip
daily wagers by the hour

26.   Grackles

the tweets grackles share, how tough that day spent
at dusk, straight, steady lines powered on poles—
hear heartbeats; rock, and roll thru clawed soles
a congregation croons intermittent

in texts they speak; that flow of keen accent
they know; how free they are, without paroles
that life strings passing through choked buttonholes
after sunset, there's respite in descent

chiffon black tides hovering— parking lots
an opera performs in neon lights
trees columned firm, extend arms big as homes

leftovers pecked; vehicles snoozed in slots
for whom boughs roll soft beds, those saved from nights
birds fly, roads walk folks, knot them with outcomes

27. Beetle

beetle on a leaf
the river wild— it's okay
hope tied to a twig

28. Uncle Darrin

Demoted, Detained, Deferred
promotion Delayed: uncle Darrin
dropped from school, never bothered
his brother made it to Harvard Law School

what not he tried, to feel the tug
hair ponytailed today, and a week later
shaven head with a blonde lock in the mid
tattooed parrots perched on his neck

one day, he bought a scratch-off ticket
bachelor aged 55, with no clue what to do
a jackpot winner—that is Destiny
he owns a dozen Diners in Dallas

29. Mocking Bird

My friend Zach, what he says, I quote:

job is all about the boss
of taking down notes, following orders
as if his offbeat ideas are innovations
laughing at stale jokes, faking awe

at his win-win stories umpteenth time
forging smiles, showing those he dislikes
are my enemies, and imitating him ditto
in choice of music, menus, books,

movies, buzzwords, and even romance
truly so—I am a Mocking bird.
So much like him, I cost much less—Guess?
CEO has swapped the boss with me

30. Jillana

picture
stone age, caves, bows and arrows
roaring hunger, sun ablaze, starry nights
nudity generalized

picture
menswear to mountain bikes, how
sky-clad Jillana fuels fantasies
totem, taboo, genderized

picture
women rights now

31. Blue Whale

as she was a standard deviation
exceeding hourglass measurements
he duffed her—blue whale

She invented her kind of revenge:

chubby, tubby, fatty checks signed
pending bills paid, skinnies out of bounds
Casio lives with Betty

She duffs him—whale-pecked

32. Sepphora, Quite Contrary

Sepphora, my Bff nicknamed Pretty Woman
believes in: Eat, Live, Love. So, she says—

Here you go to https://www.com
a video link pops on the screen
—a dot on the straight-line flickers, menu
opens: potions, lotions, herbs, and serums
buy one get one free: add to cart, add, add
Big-Discounts—beauty lies in quick fixes

try another https:// link, strike a deal
buy one, get one free on your doorstep
a bottle as large as thirst, with a king's meal
the diet and the fight; match your zeal
to eat but not in excess and to know
the vowel between drink and drunk

I don't want to be, disguised pretty—all
it takes—a facewash—without mascara
liner, lashes, powder, paints, the glow
if it doesn't show on my freckled face
if he whom I love wants me dolled up
know then that love doesn't deserve me

33. Uncle Ben

worn-out boots, socks freehold
faded jeans matching sweater
old navy overcoat lapped
he holds a book half-closed
—tired eyes decline to cope
horn-rimmed glasses hide

perils trapped in hollows
—how he misses her: to sleep
is to dream in bits—wheezes
interrupt recalls— thin gold band
glitters on a twig—bony hands
slightly shiver, the book falls

Uncle Ben, shall we go?
wrapping half-eaten sandwich
and a cookie saved in his pocket
mustering strength from left-overs
slowly, he grabs his cane
walks out of the bookstore

34. Emma

here is Emma, step-sister of grandma
her favorite dishes are spicy beans and fried okra

she drinks all kinds of cola, sinks onto her sofa
off and on, she burps, and when she farts

she laughs, showing slimy stuff stuck in her teeth
then pats her cat, who paws her doodle doo belly

Ellisa dear thinks it is a funny game
she claps and twirls and says: Nano, do it again

35. Phantom and Opera

Yes, I am lucky
no heartbreaks

no surprises
mine, mine, mine

loyal and loving
no questions asked

my two dogs
Phantom and Opera

36. Albert

placards wave at passing vehicles
it has been weeks without a shower
his childhood mowed—mauled in foster care
a mauve rose acid touched—Albert
finds shelter under the overpass

dart rail linking stations
green and red lines snaking tunnels
sunken gaze—beseeching, palms hesitating
pushcart puzzling about where to go
even in rush hours—invisible

back in kindergarten, he drew
a house, a tree, a pet, an ideal family
because he wanted to and couldn't
without unearthing his dreams
shrinks have labeled him: Loner-loser

37.   Gold

loved ones who leave us
like gold set in veins of rocks
they stay in our hearts

38. Ali Sadpara

the sun felt but still not seen
waves swiping colorless shores
—passing through a corridor
shiny dust glistening moist
on jocund flowers—an ecstasy

in treks far beyond the mark
mountaineers lost in a blizzard
flags pegged on the highest peaks
Himalayas, Karakorum and Pamir
waving, wishing, waning

as warmth recedes in faint glows
familiar faces, one fading after another
in saving others, metal sheets of ice
cloaking his life, another expedition
seems just begun

—nightly winds dance and sing
challey aao pahaaroon ki qassam
(Come back! for promises made to mounts)
homing on a star above Naga Parbat
Ali Sadpara shines over the Alps

39. Janice

famine struck once again
wandering in the barren fields: another
swollen belly in curved limbs

she joined the dying pilgrim
counting deaths, a pastime
in waiting were vultures flapping wings

too late arrived the ration sack
when emptied, they packed her in
dusted with flour

were her remains—in death, she lives
in her photo—Janice leads
      n*o kid hungry* campaigns

40. Twins

demon and dervish posed for photos
printouts were such the photog failed
to tell them both who was who

dervish was sure he was the demon
demon sure as he was the dervish
each got what he thought was him

for devotees, his photo was a lucky charm
devil, most vain, proud of how he looked
on his ID was stamped dervish

and in mirror imaging saints, those chosen
addled sinners—how robbers rob— how
some rulers' rule; our leaders lead

—uncanny resemblances

41. Grandparents

that's a rare photo of grandpa and granny
after the vows, country music played
first steps on the dancing floor

a long journey

the route from sable hair aging white
in fortunes gone, harbors lost to quandaries
they held each other

lanterns in the dark

42. Crowd

it has been days
vigils, candles, prayers
from shrines of suffering

shadows lost in the crowd walk
setting fires to cool off hurt
to protest a knee-on-neck life loss

anonymity provokes open-house pillage
breaking in stores, gathering booties
deprivation speaks aloud

rubber bullets raining
pepper balls up in the air
teargassed

mannequins, stumble-fall
Get used to it; some people say
Should I? That's the question.

43.   Sattar Edhi Baba

rich be rich but sharing a bit of wealth
        letting others live
how can that be unprofitable?

to mend hearts, to wipe fears from teary eyes
Edhi Baba, whose palms are begging bowls
        he rescues those left on roads to die

don't cheat, don't lie, don't steal, don't kill
what he says, if that taught in every school
        none can be left behind

if you stop by his place
offer a token of godsends, even a dime
        can fetch a fortune of content

44. Michael

pubs blinking festive lights
bottles pop Friday spirits
within ebbs and flows of music played
starved strings of the guitar
rhyme—

it's a paid night
for the weekend soloist
dollar bills tipped in a beer mug
last week counted less than ten
loads tied to his feet, these

curses pinned in unpaid bills
if only the guitar, a hammer
mess-ups nailed in a single hit
if only, like instant coffee, life fixed
if only, if only, if only

if only if only
that is Michael's Opioid

45. Sunflowers

yellow waves of wondrous light
blowing kisses to dispersed clouds
hazel eyes spill seeds of shine

bouquets of beige in green gold
petals walk the glowing sol
metaphors from galactic tides

fire fashioned in Gothic frames
gilded discs replicating the sun
solar shells ladling delight

as eyes swill all hues
soothing swirls of incertitude
cuddling jaded nerves

Van Gogh's sunflowers
are Prozac
for anyone, any time

46. Card Players

herding sheep, his shaggy dog is blind
wild steed, badly hurt, unfit to saddle
penurious pockets growing pores
shoes tack termite taken floors
the tired elbows rest on a day's labor
as problems pickle in a bottle of ale

wrists on table wrestle mind games
kings and queens insinuate moves
clubs and spades, with glints of red
jack on the move, eyes smoking silence
snows this year overslept over greens
farms will harvest hunger, it seems

two men sit stilted with constraints
knowing being deft is least enough to win
soil stuck in nails; palms smell of grains
choices gawk back, black and blank
jokers relax as nil in placements
no bets made; no cash laid

no battles lost; no citadels flagged
itching finger-tips measure small steps
the grimy grip on so-called trump cards
hands hold greasy diamond hearts
hoping for miracles, living in despair
it's an escape; Paul Cézanne contrives

47. Molly

penthouse styled with panache
curtains, carpets gold-threaded
Monet mounted on panels, Juliet silk
lilies in sterling silver vases, diamond
jewelry hugged in velvet cases
in stocks & bonds, her riches stored

smiles spread on glossy pages
alliances signed; headlines raved
crowds cheering screen goddess
awards received; the envy earned
designer suits, suitcases, accessories
a fashion icon was cousin Molly

beeline fans are still there
suitors keen to tie knots, yet alone
BP checked; chest filled with pills
her room, four walls, the fifth a ceiling
almost always, a made-up doll
she lives in a gift box

48. Forbes List

sun reduced to a dime
not worth candies I can buy
thinking I'll toss it in the water
with Cupid peeing in the fountain
I am not sure what to wish

love or riches or fame
that's a multiple-choice question
the first bright star appears
many others shine, their luster
worth galaxies of Kohinoor

I catch them in my eyes
count as many, make me a billionaire
then they fade, bankrupt the sky
me, a waning crescent, I carry
with me, the harvest moon

in life wanting so much
awake or asleep, if I downsize
my desires__ put needs on a treadmill
I am, let me confess modestly
the richest on the Forbes list

49. Histograms

histograms show a city mounted on a graph
stormy grey clouds perched on skyscrapers
pillars of isolation stand at 90 degrees
friendless patios braving bipolar weather
elevators pass through the curtained glass

penthouses to down below are inmates
barely talking, not even to themselves
towering flat-chest avenues, yawning
at night, quadrilateral lights watch
looming shadows befriending ghosts

brown bags binned; TV screened black
unpaid bills stacked; cell phones de-stressed
whacked bundles, put to bed, logged off
so schooled are dogs inside our bodies—
unleashed, they howl, run wild in dreams

filled with gravel and steel, in the bars
of connectivity is wired isolation, condos
converted airtight vaults are not homes
in hives piled one on another, bees
never complain; they embrace hierarchies

on skewers of compliance, every day
pushed against the columns of linearity
baby dolls, dandy boys, hooked on dating apps
uptown spas, diesel gyms, hop-daddy getaways
life stays vertical, lonely, unloved, and sad

50. Chocolates

how did love treat me
chocolates crushed in my mouth

in the ease and tease

of taste, tongue, teeth, jaws, my heart
melted smooth and softly ceased

51. Alijah

tossing caps in Nittany air
tight hugs, a degree—his imprimatur
for solo flights, nosedives, scuba drives
anything is possible

on ice-carpeted road
traffic signal freezing green, the speed
smashing windshields spread shards
stained crimson red

knee-deep wounds to last a life
the days, frozen in space and time
and miles ahead debris, strewn thick
—nightmares trapped Alijah

52.   Alijah and Amy

crawling on the floor
small hands grab the window rail
up and up, on her feet, she stands
the bars where they end, she falls
nose bruised; lips swelled bluish red

the first and second steps, unsteady
third a little less, on fourth, she fumbles
the fifth, a bit stable, *ooh, aah*, she
walks towards him: papa, papa
in winning claps, Amy coos

watching stepwise, her resolve
and himself confined to a wheelchair
long after the road mishap
my brother Alijah learns to walk
catch life step by step

53. Anne

she, wearing sunrise
sand glistening on her body
eyes wide open as her lips

young girl in her teens
her feet smelling of the sea
hair combed by the wind

shy looking Anne
mystery man, who was he
how he loved, shows on her

morning joggers stop
watch waves diminish footprints
string around her neck stays

54. Picasso Paints Pandemic

spouting blue tones of green
sable sky bruised by stars
—pale helpless nights
bleeding in eye-dews
eerie orange dawns watch
taxiing on purple brooms
witches brew tawny spells
—in grey chants

lotuses wilt in foggy pools
pink sepals faint in fumes
ogres puff brown weed, street
lamps choke murky beige
trapped lives tip-toeing
thru near-future-past-tense
sighs whisk away stories
from hospice beds, suppose

sleep gets deep on the vent
I'll drift away a memory
but if I wake up tomorrow
—escape the sorcery
pandemic erased from my easel
canvas bleached silver, with gold-
lined clouds dipped in rainbows
—I'll paint life beautiful

55. So Many Names

no fire broke, nor sun blistered rash
a gust blew through terraces of resolve
smoke swishing fumes of virus
thunder lit salvos subdued foothills
on listless roses, butterflies fell
ash rained on shriveled vineyards

crowned sparrows singed fences
phantom breeze condoled the fallen
so many names, cemeteries can tell
Ezekiel, Sheba, Deepak, Sukhdev, Justin
Hiroshi, Zach, Levant, Natasha, Jackie
Mona and Sophia: no birthdays for them

Mr. Coleman, whose dog had blue eyes
Randall, the plumber with a gold tooth
Cynthia, who lived next door, baked velvet cakes
Maxwell and Nigel, both fans of PlayStation
Tyson, the IT man; Jamila, who wrote love poems
and many more.   All vaped by Pandemic

56. Myra

V- necked blouse with laced sleeves
matching tulle skirt princess ensemble
two-tier veil and tiara Swarovski crystals
pearl laced ivory sandals, Myra,
my paternal cousin looks stunning

I do, I do, cold feet and fidgety sleep
aunt Nina served tea with lime & honey
I feel good; patting ruffled hair, she beamed—
Dr. Jacob assured no worries, just a swab test
bouquet cascading peach pink florets

the organ plays Richard Wagner
jewel of youth, proceed, there's no sorrow
no weeping nor pain, love so pure be your abode
dearly beloved, amid prayers, amid adieus
Covid-19 carries another bride

57.   Earthquake 2/6/2023

asleep, dreaming what tomorrow
will unfold; tremors lock lives in a night
everlasting—beds stagger, pillows
drop, ceilings sinking in sand clouds

rubble peaks massif—trapped
in faint-fade folds, seismic theories
nor faith-based myths can justify
why death hums aloud; why

ravenous waters swallow shores
rain-starved farms reap mud as food
like locusts, plagues shroud towns; bad
happens, and to reason why

when prayers queue, tongue-tried chants
pause in disbelief; who would for a wink
let Gog-Magog free —let them rip olive
grooves, claw-in deep, and gashes

left as slithering ravines over miles
what no mortal war could do; in a finger's
snap, a flash no nuke can dare, in a shiver
date, time, year erased

head and heart hazed as wet wood smoke
her body both a womb and Pompeii tomb
eccentric mother earth repents— piercing
is the cry—of a baby born— in debris

58. Sci-fi Film

a convoy continues in smog, time ends
the bright world around us no more exists
and high-rise cities thatched in thick soot mists
blind hostage sun—brown auburn storm descends

last world war ends, fire till the poles extends
when scrolls from scriptures sync with scientists
then death is man's act; rogue syndrome assists
red venoms pass through epochs; dusk transcends

cosmic debris hits iced rocks; rays spark sears
those sad stars out there who wish to swap lives
a wave stirs deep down; sprouts seed out of dares

who claims the earth; whales, dinosaurs, or bears
perchance, a hope; humanoid shape revives
what if it happens—sci-fi film draws scares

59. Pearls

no tooth fairy brings a gift
puts it under the pillow, when
razor sharp wrinkles split mirrors

cavities silver filled, refuse
to relish stew or soup or noodles
mouth gurgles out a red morsel

half a tooth or more falls
Marjorie picks remnants from the sink
wrap them in silk, put them

next to pearls in her jewelry box
a body in a casket, that's how she imagines
—dotage—death, my mentor-poet-friend

60. Miracle

for joys lost in her
rainbows held in fists, he came
with sunshine eyes, he saved her

Praised be Lord for prayers heard
after miscarriage, a miracle
Hakan born to Farah and Tony

61. Hakan

monitor picks little snores
sideways he turns for a while
fists rubbing eyes, he wakes up
looks around: where is papa?
oogo, boogo, pa, pa, pa
—soother slides down the bib

he coos and cries, sounding
mama, momo, maa, maa—she
picks him up, her arms latched
after the feed—the toot and burp, diaper
changed and kissed on chubby cheeks
a miracle in the cradle rocks

62.   Dad

candy kisses on my forehead drive
away dreads, in his embrace, is home

he shields me from the bad in good

helps me find the good in bad
none in the world like my dad

63. Mom

flour-dusted fingers
kneading doughs with sweet flavors

nails, glazed strawberries

her palms adding softness to pies
kiss feeding hands, that's my mom

64.   Mama's Shirt

often, she baked brownies, and if by chance
edges burnt; those sad smiley eyes credited
Kismet—since dad retired, medical bills ran
pages— mom labored jobs, tired she'd sit

some who left for dreams, their ferries sank
at least we have each other in maelstroms
the moon knows more about breakdowns
may Kismet be kind; that was her prayer

but failure weighs heavy; to ease oneself
to escape, withdraw, reconcile, be content
mind loads misfortunes on dress hangers
unfulfilled usually kept neat in closets

the voyage of a crescent is my provocation
I wish I fall off my cliffhanger, wear mama's
shirt, style it anew, scrape burns from brownies
buff old mirror, see how Kismet catwalks me

65. Odd Couple

they lived happily
ever after each brawl, each

edging precipice

each hating the other quite
secretly, love was enough

66. Crescent Eyes

imprecations: may someone push you down
the bridge, you wake up paralyzed, your place
burns to ash, your wishes turn trash, cusses

salivating tongue; your dog chews your ear
your hair dryer brings you death, a homeless
drunk rips your throat, chasing thieves, may

cops shoot you down; may you have the worst
of cancer, may you never sleep; the night brings
chest pains, your fortunes drain; you end up

on roads begging at signals —visualizing
nemesis for one once loved but lost in arguments
because I was headstrong, and he, a bit more

to forget—when someone moves out, call it quits
disappear, fades off screen; relief is in riddance
years later, you hear so, and so died—by reflex,

a part of you that still retains that bitter taste
seems suddenly gone, rage felt, hurt still there
but mellowed with time, the urge to let go

forgiveness is a prayer heard, but to share
this moment with one gone, who can't respond
that's a curse Crescent eyes must carry lifelong

67. Downside

a heart for a heart
bathed in silver, the night still
Ruth and Rex signed pacts

none but the shades watched
how inviting the desires
reckless eyes shut close

dreams dawned with a downside
expectations failed to match
pacts suffered impacts

68. Rex and Ruth

silence had an eloquence
they talked for several hours
and never said a word

starters lay cold on plates
ice melting in glasses
it fogged heartburns

vases held roses, the wilted
looked like her, and wicks
shedding tears

on each side, a menu
of accusations, dinner served
that was how a table shared

first, she got up
he followed; the door closed
outside traffic flowed as usual

I sat there wondering
my best friends Rex and Ruth
as a couple, they looked great

69.   Silverware

long winter
ditto summer
spring an interlude
in love-years
are seasons

living together
luster dulls, but

in rubs and scrubs
the stains removed
silverware shines
shines again —
(love) as good as new

70.   Guru says:

a dab of butter
even less

a touch of honey
spread evenly

on your toast
no fancy add-ons

for love to stay long
outlive, outlast

whom you love, love
daily the way you diet

71. First Love

first love, first kiss, passion held why so long
desire as bees' lips sealed on nectar canes
draw near, hug me tight— let the kiss prolong

far down in hearts, flutters rush past in throng
the first kiss draws drapes; love blindfolds all panes
first love, first kiss, passion held why so long

the fuss about that right and that so wrong
what makes sense; love is love; it never wanes
draw near, hug me tight— let the kiss prolong

to think no more but feel great, get along
and hand in hand; you, me, and moonlit lanes
first love, first kiss, passion held why so long

the sun asleep stars composing our song
as waves hum, musing on the beach are cranes
draw near, hug me tight— let the kiss prolong

in love, for love, my love, our love so strong
let there be some fires, tremors, hurricanes
first love, first kiss, passion held why so long
draw near, hug me tight— let the kiss prolong

72. Pearl Earring

She wears a pearl earring—looks somewhat shy.
Chest heaves desire—hmm! count impossible
He paints; she sits, her gray-blue, brown eyes pry.

If years pass, beauty emulates the sky
star-specked face; would she last— be visible?
She wears a pearl earring— looks somewhat shy.

a heart-shaped hope hurt through default knows why
do moon shades dark, downcast—invisible?
He paints; she sits, her gray-blue, brown eyes pry.

The rags to riches tale— sure, one can try
a girl with turbaned dreams, hmm! possible—
She wears a pearl earring—looks somewhat shy.

His hands are studio-styled, wet paints dry.
Hmm! colors blend— make art incredible.
He paints; she sits, her gray-blue, brown eyes pry.

Bright gritty gems she wants, can fate comply?
Grand sale, last act, are cheap deals credible?
She wears a pearl earring— looks somewhat shy.
Trinkets she bought pierce earlobes; *Sage eyes Scry*

73. Doorway

the place I live, thorns grow there, by the way
Cacti sprout flowers, harsh winds drift unbound
no silken rug is there in my doorway

if you expect stars dare shape your stairway
then sky must fall to fit my weathered ground
the place I live, thorns grow there, by the way

me sowing hopes to reap your smiles one day
if your eyes sidetrack, your feet slip around
no silken rug salves you in my doorway

this life is not some staged act, some screenplay
your heart in mine, but shadows that surround
the place I live, thorns grow there, by the way

that fate can help you find true love someday
to wait that long, suffer when dreams rebound
no silken rug awaits in my doorway

decide, but this time, think tough, anyway
in doubt or fear, be with me, stay profound
the place I live, thorns grow there, by the way
no silken rug—you walk in—my doorway

74. Journey by Jeep

the journey dusts around the Jeep
it's sunset—twilights blink, horns bleep
across the corner, lost sheep bleat
U-turns are sudden, sharp, and steep

I take a break—sit, savor, seep
in crispy cold air—goosebumps creep
secrets wrinkled in gravel pleat
bugs buzzing ears—woods snore asleep

worms— glow, birds, nest-wrapped; blind bats peep
the moon hides what it seeks—knee-deep
in frets, in threats, years brick retreat
to self-curb qualms—smiles plan upkeep

when wheels turn, miles whirl, bygones sweep
promises not kept hurt deep, deep
brakes screech, road claws, bruises hoofbeat
—save dreams before they die in sleep

75. Isabelle

almost all her life spent
running after shadows
vague, confused, and unclear
no pause, no stop, no rest

running, rushing, chasing
how years went by, how oaks aged
what spurred Isabelle to move on
the search for self continues

though she never looks back
a host of shadows follow her
running, rushing, chasing
nearing her, as she pauses

shadows— each one seems her
it's an existential crisis, her therapist
confides: You'll get over, how and when
only shadows can tell

76.   Sushi Lover

neck down till spine, an orchard
burgeoning—red sores ripening, oozing
sandy pains; wild berries dangle on fatigued
tendons—any cure, Jacqueline asks
                              her sister says
just pray: wait and see; the oncologists' hope
FDA will approve the drug and hooded one
wolved in woods—time, she doesn't have

Terminal, the word grasped and fully
understood, let supper be memorable—
she wears a chic dress—auburn, curly hair
let loose; south sea pearls
                    adorn an aching
wrist; a glint in her eyes scoops a world
as she sits, a waiter serves; the pianist plays
soft— bamboo chopsticks pick puffer fish

flakes soak in soya sauce and each bite
tongue kissed, it's a delicacy a chef knows
how much, how less required in a recipe
for mercy killing
                    in murky, muddy waters
wounds submerge at night; wait as stars dim
in bursts of morn, in the first glimmer of gold
sushi pink lotuses bloom neck to spine in a pond

77. Masks and Me

afraid inside, the struggle, soul, and skin
distress, it slits my selves, split seams, I hem
a lot composed and seldom scant mayhem
my looks blend sight, sound, angst, and song akin

a digit rounds none in each random spin
perhaps, in mind, strings knit hallowed anthem
dusk through dawn, shadows whittling Eve's emblem
the mirror, whom it sees, are they, my twin?

is that a crowd or lonely selves; I there
Anima, Animus: both realms ashore
tired ghosts swarm dwindling lanes: who knows me here?
—in sands are relics—some dark tales, folklore

Houdini spell frees us and from here-where—
those truths men know; our masks hide even more

78. Sheba, Sybil and Sappho

in pencil or platform heels, sprinters, or sandals
my dress, strapless, half-sleeved, or fully covered

in skintight jeans or wide pants, in skirts or gowns
in veils from the east or scarves wrapped in west

no matter what I wear and wear not, I am tagged
thus, I tick the gender box and confirm—a woman

hair dyed or not, short, long, wavy, or pin curled
regardless of eye shades used, brows plucked, or not

tilt of nose; width of my lips; cheekbones high or not
dimpled smile or usual, the neck held straight or bent

shoulder blades with arms spread like angel wings
I animate inspirations; my images style art

heart sandwiched between mellowed swells
tummy tucked or not, how much swing or sway

bumps sloping down, legs—slender, shapely, or not
supple feet like silver bells in slipping sands

I, me, walk prose, adding folders on desktops
Sheba, Sybil, and Sappho micro-craft outlooks

fastened in gold and silver, and platinum chains
bracelets—sapphire studded—such shiny gems

emeralds, rubies, Akoya pearls fitted in rings
ears pierced and diamonds secured in nose pins

charms tingling anklets, and such ornaments
to make me feel special, yes, I am obliged

to think, I am bound, moored in metals—seized
that's an illusion infused in He-fables, fairytales

my mind is where the multiverse conceived
for fortune-tellers, I fashion poems in auguries

my bounce has no shorelines and sky unending
as changing moon, a bright star: I sign woman

piecemeal campaigns appear, appeal, and fade
I am not a placard, not a symbol, not a shout

my photo smiles are sweet-nothings like knives
no gambit can handcuff my rights, deter me

medieval-thinking days are over—now I design
my labels; straighten witchy flames 90 degrees

I am here not to compete or complain or explain
the way I am, because of who I am, I am so sure

because I am a woman; I prefix man; he suffixes me
two distinct circles overlapping in the Ven diagram

you stay as you and me as me—the more we share
imagine how not this world transforms

79. Last Photo

the last page of my album is blank
how about a selfie of you and me?
whatever our differences, the said unsaid
and suffered—after years lost in hesitations
after seasons of uncertainties

not knowing what regrets await
in twilights far beyond, pretend clouds
are mountains and on the tallest peaks
we sing full throttle our favorite songs
pretend—where we live

neath gardens, streams flow
of milk and honey and drinks so many
our souls savor sups in glows
in sweet consent and bliss thus known
that photo—I want it with you

Dr. Rubeena Anjum, a recipient of the Hubert Humphrey Fellowship at Pennsylvania State University (2007-08), started her career as a news Sub-Editor in The Pakistan Times, Rawalpindi. In the Pakistan Air Force, she was the first lady commissioned officer in the Education Branch and served as a psychologist. Her commitment to providing quality education to girls enabled her to establish Garrison Academy for Girls and Garrison Academy for Cambridge Studies, two renowned educational institutions in Lahore. Throughout her career, she remained associated with editing newsletters and literary magazines. Now retired, she enjoys traveling and pursues her passion for reading and writing poetry. Her favorite cities are Lahore, Istanbul, and Dallas. She is a member of the Richardson Poets Group and Dallas Poets Community. Her work has appeared in *The Ekphrastic Review, The Bosphorus Review of Books, Artistic Antidote UMN Clinical Affairs, Corona Virus Anthology* by Austin International Poetry Festival 2020, *Art on the Trails: Mending 2021 Chapbook, Word City Literary Journal, Southwestern American Literature, The Writer's Garret-Common Language Project: Networks Anthology 2023*, among others published in Pakistan.

www.ingramcontent.com/pod-product-compliance
Lightning Source LLC
Chambersburg PA
CBHW031124160426
43192CB00008B/1109